INTRO

CW01501776

This book is a pocket refere
saltwater fish that are pres
Britain.

Colour illustrations are provided together with brief information on the distribution of each species.

The little book of British sea fish is one of a series of small reference guides designed to take up very little room in a pocket or backpack, but still provide enough information to identify the flora and fauna of Britain.

This book is also available for the Amazon Kindle and other electronic readers such as tablets and mobile phones using the Amazon Kindle app.

ALMACO JACK
Seriola rivioliana

A rare fish in british waters, the almaco jack is more commonly found in the Pacific and Carribean.

ANCHOVY
Engraulis encrasicolus

The anchovy is widely distributed throughout the world's oceans where they swim in large shoals.

The Little Book of British Sea Fish

PAUL DUFFIELD

CONTENTS

ANGLER FISH
Lophius piscatorius

The angler fish is present all around the British Isles. It is most common on the west coast of England, Scotland and Wales and the north, south and east coasts of Ireland.

ARGENTINE
Argentina sphyraena

The argentine, also known as the herring smelt, are found throughout the world's oceans.

BARRACUDINA
Paralepis coregonoides

Fish of the barracudina family are found throughout the world's oceans, most often in deep waters.

BASS
Dicentrarchus labrax

The bass is found in waters around Europe including the Atlantic and Mediterranean and is present all around the British Isles.

BLACKFISH
Centrolophus niger

The blackfish is found in all tropical and temperate oceans at depths up to 1,000 metres.

BLACKFISH (CORNISH)
Schedophilus medusophagus

The Cornish blackfish is found in tropical and temperate oceans, usually at depths over 200 metres.

BLENNY (BUTTERFLY)
Blennius ocellaris

The butterfly blenny is found in the oceans of northern and western Europe, as well as the Mediterranean and Black Sea. It is present in the English Channel and Irish Sea.

BLENNY (TOMPOT)
Parablennius gattorugine

The tompot blenny is found in the oceans of northern and western Europe, the Mediterranean and Black Sea.

BLENNY (VIVIPAROUS)
Zoarces viviparus

The viviparous blenny is found in the north east Atlantic including seas such as the Baltic, Irish, and North seas.

BLENNY (YARRELL'S)
Chirolophis ascanii

The Yarrell's blenny is widely distributed and is found in the Atlantic ocean, around the British Isles, Orkneys, Faroes and Shetland Isles.

BLUEMOUTH
Helicolenus dactylopterus

The bluemouth, also known as the bluemouth rockfish is widely distributed throughout the Atlantic and Mediterranean.

BLUE RUNNER
Caranx crysos

The blue runner is widely distributed throughout the Atlantic and Mediterranean.

BOAR FISH
Capros aper

The boar fish is found in the Atlantic and Mediterranean and is present off the southwest costs of Britain and Ireland.

BOGUE
Boops boops

The bogue is found in the Atlantic, Mediterranean and Black Sea.

BONITO
Sarda sarda

The Bonito is common in the Atlantic, Mediterranean, and Black Sea.

BREAM (AXILLARY)
Pagellus acarne

The axillary bream, also known as the spanish bream is found in the Atlantic and Mediterranean. It is rare in the British Isles but are occasionally caught off the south coast of England.

BREAM (BLACK)
Spondyliosom cantharus

The black bream is present in northern European waters and the Mediterranean. It is found off the south coast of England.

BREAM (COUCH'S SEA)
Pagrus pagrus

The Couch's sea bream is present in the Atlantic and Mediterranean. It is found off the south coast of England.

BREAM (GILTHEAD)
Sparus aurata

The gilthead bream is present in the Atlantic and Mediterranean. It is found off the south coast of England.

BREAM (PANDORA)
Pagellus erythrinus

The pandora bream is present in the Atlantic, Mediterranean and North Sea. It is found off the south coast of England.

BREAM (RAY'S)
Brama brama

The Ray's bream is present in the Atlantic, Indian and Pacific Oceans. It is found off the south coast of England.

BREAM (RED)
Pagellus bogaraveo

The red bream is present in the Mediterranean, Atlantic and Pacific Oceans. It is found off the south coast of England.

BREAM (SADDLED SEA)
Oblada melanura

The saddled sea bream is present in the Atlantic and Mediterranean. It is found off the south coast of England.

BREAM (WHITE SEA)
Diplous sargus

The white sea bream is present in the Atlantic, Mediterranean and Black Sea. It is found off the south coast of England.

BRILL
Scophthalmus rhombus

The Brill is present in the Atlantic, Mediterranean and Black Sea. It is found around the costs of Britain and Ireland but are more common in the south.

BULL HUSS
Scyliorhinus stellaris

The bull huss is present in the Atlantic and Mediterranean and is found throughout Britain and Ireland from the Shetland Isles to the coasts of Cornwall.

BUTTERFISH
Pholis gunnellus

The butterfish is present in the Atlantic, North Sea, White Sea and Baltic Sea.

CATFISH
Anarhichas lupus

The catfish is present in the Atlantic, Mediterranean and Baltic Sea and is found on the north coasts of England and Scotalnd.

COALFISH
Pollachius virens

The coalfish, also known as the saithe, is present in the eastern and western Atlantic and is found all around the British Isles.

COD
Gadus morhua

The cod is present in the northern and western Atlantic and Arctic and is found all around the British Isles.

COMBER
Serranus cabrilla

The comber is present in the Atlantic, Mediterranean and Black Sea..

CONGER
Conger conger

The conger eel is widely distributed around the British Isles.

DAB
Limanda limanda

Dab are present in Atlantic, Baltic and White Sea. It is present all round Britain and Ireland, particularly the North Sea.

DAB (LONG ROUGH)
Hippoglossoides platessoides

Long rough dab are present in the eastern and western Atlantic.

DOGFISH (BLACK-MOUTHED)
Galeus melastomus

Black mouthed dogfish are present in the Atlantic and Mediterranean.

DOGFISH (LESSER SPOTTED)
Scyliorhinus canicula

The lesser spotted dogfish is present in the Atlantic and Mediterranean and are common around the coasts of Britain and Ireland.

DRAGONET
Callionymus lyra

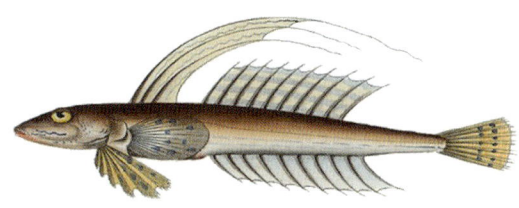

The dragonet is present in the Atlantic, Mediterranean, Black Sea, Aegean and Adriatic Sea, Azores and the Canary Islands. It is widespread around the coasts of Britain and Ireland.

FLOUNDER
Pleuronectes flesus

The flounder is present in the Atlantic, Mediterranean, White Sea and Black Sea and is common around the coats of Britain and Ireland.

FORKBEARD (GREATER)
Phycis blennoides

The greater forkbeard is present in the Atlantic and Mediterranean.

GARFISH
Belone belone

The garfish is present in the Atlantic and Mediterranean and is found throughout the British Isles.

GARFISH (SHORT-BEAKED)
Belone svetovidovi

The short beaked garfish is present in the Atlantic and Mediterranean.

GOBY (BLACK)
Gobius niger

The black goby is present in the Atlantic, Mediterranean, Baltic and Black Sea and is widely distributed around the British Isles.

GOBY (COMMON)
Pomatoschistus microps

The common goby is present in the Atlantic, Mediterranean and Baltic Sea and is widely distributed around the British Isles.

GOBY (GIANT)
Gobius cobitis

The giant goby is present in the Atlantic, Mediterranean and Black Sea.

GOBY (LEOPARD-SPOTTED)
Thorogobius ephippiatus

The leopard spotted goby is present in the eastern Atlantic and Mediterranean and is found around the south west coast of England.

GOBY (SAND)
Ctenolabrus rupestris

The sand goby is present in the Atlantic, Mediterranean and Black Sea. It is widely distributed throughout Britain and Ireland but rare in the North Sea.

GOBY (ROCK)
Gobius paganellus

The rock goby is present in the Atlantic, Mediterranean and Black Sea. It is found around the south and west coasts of England and Scotland and around the coasts of Wales and Ireland.

GUINEAN AMBERJACK
Seriola carpenteri

The guinean amberjack is present in the eastern Atlantic and Mediterranean.

GURNARD (GREY)
Eutrigla gurnardus

The grey gurnard is present in the Atlantic, Mediterranean and Black Sea and is found off the south and west coasts England, the west coast of Scotland, Wales and the east and south coasts of Ireland.

GURNARD (RED)
Aspitrigla cuculus

The red gurnard is present in the Atlantic, Mediterranean and Black Sea and is found throughout the British Isles.

GURNARD (STREAKED)
Trigloporus lastoviza

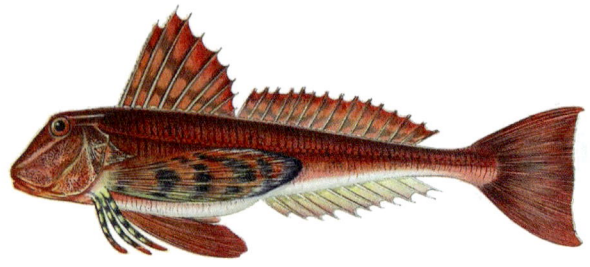

The streaked gurnard is present in the eastern Atlantic.

GURNARD (YELLOW OR TUBFISH)
Trigla lucerna

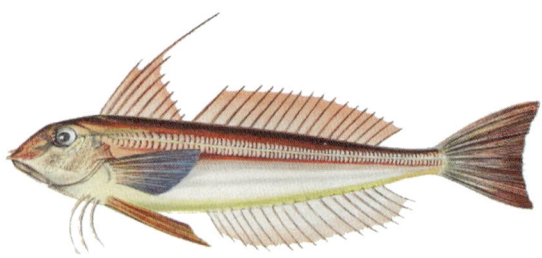

The yellow or tubfish gurnard is present in the Atlantic, Mediterranean and Black Sea.

HADDOCK
Melanogrammus aeglefinus

The haddock is present in the northeast and northwest Atlantic. It is found throughout British Isles but is more common off the north east coast of Scotland, the north east and south west coasts of England and the Irish sea.

HADDOCK (NORWAY)
Sebastes viviparus

The Norway haddock is present in the northeast Atlantic North Sea and around the Shetland Islands, Scotland, northern England, Wales and Ireland.

HAKE
Merluccius merluccius

The hake is present in the Atlantic, Mediterranean and Black Sea. It is found in the western English Channel, the Irish Sea and off southern Ireland.

HALIBUT
Hippoglossus hippoglossus

The halibut is present in the eastern and western Atlantic and is found throughout the British Isles.

HERRING
Clupea harengus

The herring is present in the north and east Atlantic and the Baltic Sea and is found in the North Sea, the English Channel and the Irish Sea.

JOHN DORY
Zeus faber

The john dory is present in the Atlantic, Pacific, Mediterranean, Black Sea and Indian Ocean and is found around all British and Irish coasts.

LING
Molva molva

The ling is present in the northeast and northwest Atlantic and the northwest Mediterranean and is found all around the British Isles, mainly off the south and west coasts of England, Ireland and the west Scotland.

LUMPSUCKER
Cyclopterus lumpus

The lumpsucker is present in the eastern and western Atlantic. It is found throughout Britain and Ireland but rarely off the south coast of England.

MACKEREL
Scomber scombrus

The mackerel is found in the Atlantic and North Sea and western British Isles.

MACKEREL (SPANISH)
Scomber japonicus

The spanish mackerel is present in the Atlantic, Red Sea and northern Indian Ocean.

MEGRIM
Lepidorhombus whiffiagonis

The megrim is present in the northeast Atlantic and western Mediterranean.

MONKFISH
Squatina squatina

The monkfish is present in the Atlantic, Mediterranean and Black Sea. It is mainly found off the west coast of England, Wales and Scotland and the north, south and east coasts of Ireland.

MULLET (GOLDEN GREY)
Liza aurata

The golden grey mullet is present in the Atlantic, Mediterranean and Black Sea. Found throughout the UK, but more common in the south and west.

MULLET (RED)
Mullus surmuletus

The red mullet is present in the Atlantic, Mediterranean and Black Sea. Found off the south and west of England and south of Ireland.

MULLET (THICK-LIPPED GREY)
Chelon labrosus

The thick lipped grey mullet is present in the Atlantic, Mediterranean and Black Sea. Found throughout the UK, but more common in the south and west.

MULLET (THIN-LIPPED GREY)
Liza ramada

The thin lipped grey mullet is present in the Atlantic, Mediterranean and Black Sea. Found throughout the UK, but more common in the south and west.

OPAH
Lampris guttatus

The opah is present in the Atlantic, Pacific and Mediterranean.

PERCH (DUSKY)
Epinephelus marginatus

The dusky perch is present in the Atlantic, Mediterranean and Indian Ocean.

PILCHARD
Sardina pilchardus

The pilchard is present in the Atlantic, Mediterranean Adriatic and Black Sea.

PILOT FISH
Naucrates ductor

The pilot fish is present in the Atlantic, Mediterranean, Pacific and Indian Ocean.

PIPEFISH (GREATER)
Syngnathus acus

The greater pipefish is present in the Atlantic, Mediterranean, Pacific and Indian Ocean. Widely distributed along the south and west coasts of England, west coast of Scotland and the north east and south coasts of Ireland.

PIPEFISH (SNAKE)
Entelurus aequoreus

The snake pipefish is present in the Atlantic and Baltic Sea. It is found off the west coasts of England and Ireland.

PLAICE
Pleuronectes platessa

The Plaice is present in the North Sea and are common around the British Isles.

POGGE
Agonus cataphractus

The pogge is present in the northeast Atlantic, White sea and the southern Baltic. It is found in inshore waters all around Britain and Ireland.

POLLACK
Pollachius pollachius

The pollack is present in the northeast Atlantic and southern Baltic. It is found off all coasts around Britain and Ireland.

POOR COD
Trisopterus minutus

The poor cod is present in the Atlantic and Mediterranean and is common around Britain and Ireland.

POUTING (BIB, POUT)
Trisopterus luscus

The pouting is present in the eastern Atlantic and western Mediterranean and is common around Britain and Ireland.

PUFFER FISH
Lagocephalus lagocephalus

The puffer fish is present in the Atlantic, Indian, Mediterranean and Pacific.

RAY (BLONDE)
Raja brachyura

The blonde ray is present in the eastern Atlantic and is widely distributed in European waters.

RAY (BOTTLE-NOSED)
Raja alba

The bottle nosed ray is present in the eastern Atlantic and western Mediterranean. It is found off the south west coasts of Britain and Ireland.

RAY (CUCKOO)
Raja naevus

The cuckoo ray is present in the eastern Atlantic, North Sea and Mediterranean. It is mainly found off the south west coast of England and Wales but is occasionally caught off other British and Irish coasts.

RAY (EAGLE)
Myliobatis aquila

The eagle ray is present in the eastern Atlantic, southwest North Sea and throughout the Mediterranean. It is sometimes found off the coasts of south and east England and Ireland.

RAY (ELECTRIC)
Torpedo nobiliana

The electric ray is present in the eastern Atlantic and throughout the Mediterranean. It is found in the English Channel, off the west coasts of Wales and Northern Ireland and the west coast of Scotland.

RAY (MARBLED ELECTRIC)
Torpedo marmorata

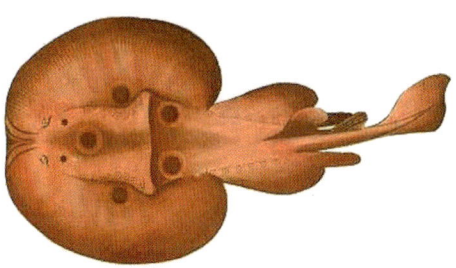

The marbled electric ray is present in the eastern Atlantic and throughout the Mediterranean. It is found in the southern North Sea, the English Channel, and along the west coast of Scotland.

RAY (SANDY)
Raja circularis

The sandy ray is present in the eastern Atlantic and western Mediterranean. It is found off the north and west coasts of Scotland, the Shetland Isles and Ireland.

RAY (SMALL-EYED)
Raja microocellata

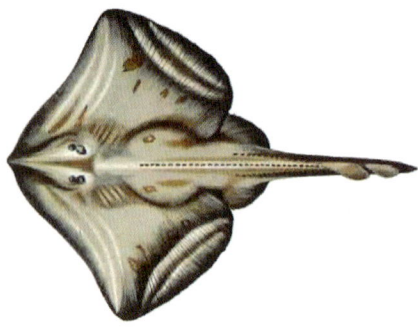

The small eyed ray is present in the Atlantic and is found off the southern and western coasts of England and most of Ireland.

RAY (SPOTTED)
Raja montagui

The spotted ray is present in the eastern Atlantic, southern North Sea, the western Baltic and western Mediterranean. It is found around most of the coasts of England and Ireland except the east coast of England.

RAY (STING)
Dasyatis pastinaca

The sting ray is present in the northeast Atlantic and Mediterranean and can be found in the English Channel and Irish Sea.

RAY (THORNBACK)
Raja clavata

The thornback ray is present in the eastern Atlantic, western Baltic, Mediterranean and Black Sea. It is common around all coasts of Britain and Ireland.

RAY (UNDULATE)
Raja undulata

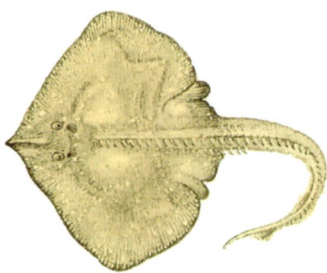

The undulate ray is present in the eastern Atlantic and western Mediterranean. It is found off the southern and western coasts of England as well as the coasts of Wales and much of Ireland.

RED BAND-FISH
Cepola rubescens

The red band fish is present in the eastern Atlantic and Mediterranean. It is found off the south west coasts of England and Wales and the south and south west of Ireland.

ROCKLING (FIVE BEARDED)
Ciliata mustela

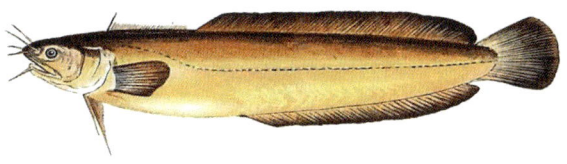

The five bearded rockling is present in the northeast Atlantic and is found around all coasts of Britain and south-east Ireland.

ROCKLING (FOUR BEARDED)
Enchelyopus cimbrius

The four bearded rockling is present in the north Atlantic and Baltic Sea. It has been found around the scottish coast.

ROCKLING (SHORE)
Gaidropsarus mediterraneus

The shore rockling is present in the eastern Atlantic and Black Sea and is found around all coasts of Britain and south east Ireland.

ROCKLING (THREE BEARDED)
Gaidropsarus vulgaris

The three bearded rockling is present in the northeast Atlantic, North Sea and northern Mediterranean.

SALMON (COHO)
Oncorhynchus kisutch

The Coho salmon is present in the Pacific and is found off the Shetland Isles and most coasts of Britain and Ireland.

SANDEEL (CORBIN'S)
Hyperoplus immaculatus

The Corbin's sandeel is present in the northeast Atlantic and is found on all coasts of the British Isles and English Channel.

SANDEEL (GREATER)
Hyperoplus lanceolatus

The greater sandeel is present in the northeast Atlantic and is widely distributed around the coasts of Britain and Ireland.

SCAD (HORSE MACKEREL)
Trachurus trachurus

The scad is present in the northeast Atlantic and Mediterranean and is found off the south west of England and the south of Ireland.

SEA SCORPION (LONG SPINNED)
Taurulus bubalis

The long spined sea scorpion is found in the eastern Atlantic and Mediterranean. It is common on all coasts of Britain and Ireland.

SEA SCORPION (SHORT-SPINED)
Myoxocephalus scorpius

The short spined sea scorpion is found in the eastern Atlantic, North Sea, Baltic Sea and Arctic Ocean. It is common on all coasts of Britain and Ireland.

SHAD (ALLIS)
Alosa alosa

The allis shad is present in the eastern Atlantic, Baltic Sea and western Mediterranean. Small numbers are found in many areas around the British Isles.

SHAD (TWAITE)
Alosa fallax

The twaite shad is present in the eastern Atlantic, Baltic Sea, Black Sea and western Mediterranean. Small numbers are found in many areas around the British Isles.

SHANNY
Lipophrys pholis

The shanny is present in the eastern Atlantic and Mediterranean and is found around south west Britain and the south coast of Ireland.

SHARK (BLUE)
Prionace glauca

The blue shark is present in all main oceans and is found in western British and Irish waters in the summer months.

SHARK (MAKO)
Isurus oxyrinchus

The mako shark is present in all main oceans and is found throughout British and Irish waters but is rare off south east Britain.

SHARK (PORBEAGLE)
Lamna nasus

The porbeagle shark is present in all main oceans and is found throughout British and Irish waters.

SHARK (SIX-GILLED)
Hexanchus griseus

The six gilled shark is present in all main oceans but is rarely found around the British Isles.

SHARK (THRESHER)
Alopias vulpinus

The thresher shark is present in all main oceans and is found around the British Isles in the summer months.

SKATE (COMMON)
Raja batis

The common skate is present in the eastern Atlantic, western Baltic and western Mediterranean. It is found in the western British Channel, off the coasts of west and north Ireland, west Scotland and the Scilly Isles.

SKIPPER
Scomberesox saurus

The skipper is widely distributed throughout many of the world's oceans. It is found off the Channel Isles and Cornish coast during the late summer months.

SMELT
Osmerus eperlanus

The smelt is present in the north Atlantic, White Sea, North Sea, and Baltic. It is found off the east coast of Britain and west coast of Scotland.

SMELT (SAND)
Atherina presbyter

The sand smelt is present in the eastern Atlantic and western Mediterranean. It is common in the North Sea and English Channel.

SMELT (SAND - BIG SCALE)
Atherina boyeri

The big scale sand smelt is present in the eastern Atlantic , Black Sea and Mediterranean. It is common in the North Sea and English Channel.

SMOOTHHOUND
Mustelus mustelus

The smoothhound is present in the eastern Atlantic and Mediterranean. It found in British waters, but is more common off the south west coast of England.

SMOOTHHOUND (STARRY)
Mustelus asterias

The starry smoothhound is present in the northeast Atlantic and Mediterranean. It found in British waters, but is more common off the south west coast of Scotland.

SOLE
Solea solea

The sole is present in the eastern Atlantic, North Sea, Black Sea and Mediterranean. It is found off west Scotland, the Irish Sea, and the welsh coast but not southern England.

SOLE (LEMON)
Microstomus kitt

The lemon sole is present in the northeast Atlantic and White Sea. Although present around the British Isles, it is rarely caught by anglers.

SPURDOG
Squalus acanthias

The spurdog is present in the western Atlantic, Black Sea and Mediterranean. It is found in coastal around most of the British Isles, but is more common off the west coasts of England, Scotland and Ireland.

STICKLEBACK (SEA 15 SPINED)
Spinachia spinachia

The 15 spined sea stickleback is present in the northeast Atlantic. It is found on all coasts of Britain and Ireland but is uncommon in the south east.

SUNFISH
Mola mola

The sunfish is present in warm and termperate zones of all the world's oceans. It is found off the coasts of Scotland and Ireland, the Irish Sea and the south and west coasts of England.

TADPOLE-FISH
Raniceps raninus

The tadpole fish is present in the northeast Atlantic and is found on all coasts of the British Isles.

TOPE
Gaeorhinus galeus

The tope is widespread in temperate waters of the world's oceans and is found all round the British Isles, but is less common in the north east.

TOPNOT (COMMON)
Zeugopterus punctatus

The topknot is present in the north Atlantic and is found in many areas around the British and Irish coast.

TORSK
Brosme brosme

The torsk is present in the northeast and northwest Atlantic and the Mediterranean. It is found around all coasts of Scotland, north-east England and north-west Ireland.

TRIGGER FISH
Balistes capriscus

The trigger fish is present in the eastern Atlantic, Pacific and Red Sea. It is found around the western coasts of Britain and Ireland.

TUNNY
Thunnus thynnus

The tunny is present in the Atlantic, Indian and Pacific oceans. It is found off the east south and south west coasts of Britain and Ireland.

TUNNY (BIG-EYED)
Thunnus obesus

The big eyed tunny is present in the Atlantic, Indian and Pacific oceans. It is rarely found in British waters.

TUNNY (LONG-FINNED)
Thunnus alalunga

The long finned tunny is present in the North Atlantic, Pacific and Indian Oceans and the Mediterranean. It is rarely found in British waters.

TURBOT
Scophthalmus maximus

The turbot is present in the northeast Atlantic, Baltic, Arctic, Black Sea and Mediterranean. It is found in many areas around the British and Irish coast.

WEEVER (GREATER)
Trachinus draco

The greater weever is present in the eastern Atlantic, North Sea and Mediterranean. It is common all round the British Isles.

WEEVER (LESSER)
Echiichthys vipera

The lesser weever is present in the eastern Atlantic, North Sea and Mediterranean. It is common all round the British Isles.

CARE SHOULD BE TAKEN WHEN HANDLING WEEVER AS THEIR SPINES SECRETE A STRONG POISON

WHITING
Merlangius merlangus

The whiting is present in the northeast Atlantic, Barents, Black, Aegean and Adriatic seas and northwest Mediterranean. It is found throughout British and Irish waters.

WHITING BLUE (POUTASSOU)
Micromesistius poutassou

The blue whiting is present in the northeast Atlantic: Barents Sea, eastern Norwegian Sea and western Mediterranean. It is found off the coasts of Scotland, south and south east England, east Wales and Ireland and the English Channel.

WITCH FLOUNDER
Glyptocephalus cynoglossus

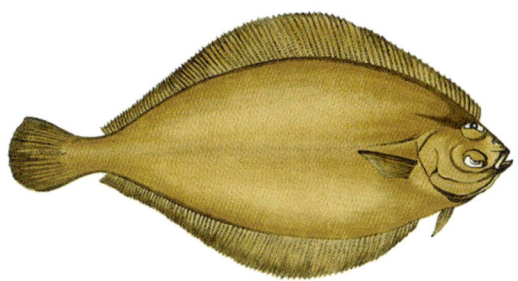

The witch flounder is present in the eastern and western Atlantic and is found throughout the British Isles.

WRASSE (BAILLON'S)
Crenilabrus bailloni

The Baillon's wrasse is present in the eastern Atlantic and Mediterranean. It is less common that other species of wrasse but can be found around much of the British and Irish coast.

WRASSE (BALLAN)
Labrus bergylta

The ballan wrasse is present in the eastern Atlantic and is common off all English and Irish coasts.

WRASSE (CORKWING)
Crenilabrus melops

The corkwing wrasse is present in the eastern Atlantic, Adriatic and Mediterranean. It is widely distributed around the British Isles, but more common in the south and west.

WRASSE (CUCKOO)
Labrus mixtus

The cuckoo wrasse is present in the eastern Atlantic and Mediterranean. It is found around most coasts of the British Isles.

WRASSE (GOLDSINNEY)
Ctenolabrus rupestris

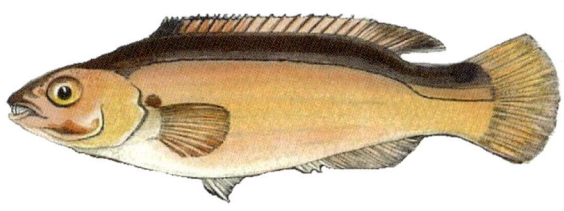

The goldsinney wrasse is present in the eastern Atlantic, Black sea and Mediterranean. It is widely distributed throughout Britain and Ireland, but rare in the North Sea and eastern Channel

WRASSE (ROCK COOK)
Centrolabrus exoletus

The rock cook wrasse is present in the eastern Atlantic. It is distributed throughout Britain and Ireland, but is not found in the southern North Sea.

WRASSE (SCALE-RAYED)
Acantholabrus palloni

The scale rayed wrasse is present in the eastern Atlantic, Adriatic and Mediterranean. While occasionally found around the British Isles, it is extremely rare.

WRECKFISH
Polyprion americanus

The wreckfish is present in the eastern and western Atlantic and Mediterranean. It is found throughout British and Irish waters with the exception of the southern North Sea.

ACKNOWLEDGMENTS

Pictures of fish used in this book are public domain images reproduced from by the artists acknowledged below and images released into the public domain by the U.S. Fish and Wildlife Service.

Jonathan Couch: Bream (Saddled Sea), Scad (Horse Mackerel), Bass, Black Fish, Blackfish (Cornish), Blenny (Butterfly), Blenny (Yarrell's), Boar Fish, Bogue, Bonito, Bream (Axillary), Bream (Black), Bream (Couch's Sea), Bream (Gilthead), Bream (Pandora), Bream (Ray's), Brill, Bull Huss, Coalfish, Cod, Comber, Conger, Dab, Dab (Long Rough), Dogfish (Black-Mouthed), Dogfish (Lesser Spotted), Flounder, Forkbeard (Greater), Goby (Common), Goby (Leopard-Spotted), Goby (Sand), Goby (Rock), Gurnard (Streaked), Gurnard (Yellow Or Tubfish), Haddock, Haddock (Norway), Hake, Halibut, Herring, John Dory, Ling, Mackerel, Megrim, Monkfish, Mullet (Golden Grey), Mullet (Thick-Lipped Grey), Mullet (Thin-Lipped Grey), Opah, Perch (Dusky), Pipefish (Greater), Pipefish (Snake), Plaice, Pollack, Ray (Bottle-Nosed), Ray (Cuckoo), Ray (Eagle), Ray (Sandy), Ray (Small-Eyed), Ray (Spotted), Ray (Sting), Ray (Thornback), Red Band-Fish, Rockling (Five Bearded), Rockling (Four Bearded), Sandeel (Corbin's), Sandeel (Greater), Shad (Allis), Shad (Twaite), Shanny, Shark (Blue), Shark (Porbeagle), Shark (Thresher), Skate (Common), Skipper, Smelt, Smelt (Sand), Smelt (Sand - Big Scale), Smoothhound, Smoothhound (Starry), Sole, Sole (Lemon), Spurdog, Stickleback (Sea 15 Spined), Sunfish, Tope, Topnot (Common), Torsk, Trigger Fish, Tunny, Turbot, Weever (Greater), Whiting, Witch, Wrasse (Baillon's), Wrasse (Ballan), Wrasse (Corkwing), Wrasse (Goldsinney), Wrasse (Rock Cook), Wrasse (Scale-Rayed) ; Marcus Bloch: Angler Fish, Blenny (Viviparous), Dragonet, Garfish, Goby (Giant), Guinean Amberjack, Gurnard (Grey), Pilchard, Puffer

Fish, Ray (Marbled Electric), Sea Scorpion (Long Spinned), Weever (Lesser); George Cuvier: Barracudina, Butterfish, Catfish, Gurnard (Red), Lumpsucker, Pogge, Ray (Undulate), Rockling (Shore), Wreckfish; einhold Thiele: Mullet (Red), Rockling (Three Bearded), Wrasse (Cuckoo); Henri Gervais: Anchovy, Argentine, Poor Cod, Pouting (Bib, Pout), Ray (Electric), Shark (Six-Gilled), Tadpole-Fish, Whiting Blue (Poutassou); Edward Donovan: Blenny (Tompot), Goby (Black); Eskrol (Wikimedia Commons): Garfish (Short-Beaked); John Edwards Holbrook: Almaco Jack; USFWS: Blue Runner, Bream (White Sea), Salmon (Coho), Tunny (Big-Eyed), Tunny (Long-Finned); V.S. Balasheva: Sea Scorpion (Short-Spined); Edgar R. Waite:Shark (Mako); Arthus Bertrand:Pilot Fish; Barton W. Everman:Mackerel (Spanish); François-Étienne de La Roche:Bluemouth; Friedrich Henle:Ray (Blonde); H. de La Blanchère:Bream (Red)

ABOUT THE AUTHOR

Paul Duffield is an author with a keen interest in the countryside.

He became interested in nature at a young age and having lived, worked, fished and walked over many parts of Britain he realised that a series of small easy to carry reference books on fish, plants, birds, insects and other animals would be ideal for anyone with an interest in the natural world.

Printed in Great Britain
by Amazon.co.uk, Ltd.,
Marston Gate.